The Ultimate Marketing Tool

How to Stand Out in the Marketplace and Eliminate Your Competition

Doug Johnson

The Ultimate Marketing Tool:

How to Stand Out in the Marketplace

And Eliminate Your Competition

Copyright © 2014 Doug Johnson

All Rights Reserved

Printed in the USA

Published by Ben Franklin Publishing Company

ISBN – 0982742738

ISBN - 978-0-9827427-3-0

Cover design services by EditWriteDesign.com

Cover image: NatUlrich/Shutterstock.com

Table of Contents

Your Competitor's Worst Fear

How would you like to have an edge on your competition that they couldn't beat? Imagine being able to stand out from them so that no matter what they do, they won't be considered in your league. Your days of fighting price competition would be virtually eliminated because customers would see you as unique among your competitors.

Is this possible? Can you get away from the constant battle of price competition and grow your business profitably?

Yes you can. And I'm here to show you how to do it.

Let me ask you a question. When you're looking to do business with someone and you have no contacts that could refer you to someone reputable, what do you do? If you're like the vast majority of people, you try to find out about businesses that offer the service or product you're looking for so that you can make an informed decision about who to do business with. But it's hard to decide when you really don't know the businesses personally.

Let's suppose you're looking for a real estate agent. In the old days you'd open the yellow pages and compare ads of different agents and try to decide which one you should call. Today we go to the internet and look at websites. We're really doing the same thing using a different format. We're looking for something that will tell us who we should consider and why they're the best choice.

And when you don't know one agent from another, it's hard to know which one to choose. Sure, you could try to gauge them by the advertisements you've seen or heard. But those don't really give you any way to compare, other than to see which real estate agent has the most persuasive advertising.

The same holds true for most any business you're trying to find. Whether it's an attorney, doctor, veterinarian, auto repair shop, plumber, electrician, chiropractor, or any other type of business, you have a hard time knowing which one to choose.

But if, for example, you were looking for an auto repair shop and you learned something unique about the owner that made them stand out compared to their competition, then you'd take notice. If he was an expert beyond the usual training that everyone advertises, the kind of expert that the industry turns to when they need a problem solved, you'd start thinking that he was the guy to take your car to for repairs. Let me give you an example.

When I was young I moved to a city to take a new job. In those days I drove foreign sports cars and they were finicky things, regularly needing service just to maintain them, let alone to fix them when something went wrong. Dealers always seemed to overcharge you and even their mechanics never seemed to get things really "right" with the cars.

I arrived in the new city on a Saturday morning with my car acting up. After I checked into my hotel (remember, I was brand new in town and didn't even have a place to live yet) I looked in the yellow pages and found a dealer whose shop was open. I took the car there, knowing I had to get it fixed right away since I was due to start my new job Monday. As I sat in the waiting room I didn't know what to expect. Finally, after waiting about 45 minutes, the shop manager came in and told me the bad news. The repairs were $1300, which was very expensive for a young guy in the 1970s. He took me out and pointed at stuff under the hood and I had no idea what he was talking about. He said I needed to get it fixed right away. Then he assured me I was in the right place because he'd have his mechanics stay as late as they needed to get it fixed for me.

I knew something was wrong with what he was telling me, but I didn't know enough about these cars to have any idea whether he was telling me the truth or not. I knew I had a problem but something just didn't feel right. I told him to take the car off the rack and I'd think about it. He warned me that I shouldn't drive it but I didn't listen to him. I only had a couple of miles to drive back to the hotel. I just wanted time to think about it.

I drove back to the hotel and didn't leave for the entire weekend. I looked at the yellow pages ads over and over again hoping that maybe I'd missed something that would tell me which shop was superior to the others. But I found nothing.

I noticed that there was a shop that specialized in the kind of car I drove. It was the only type of vehicle they worked on. I'd been to a shop like that in my old city and been burned by them. These kinds of shops knew these cars were a bit exotic and some of them took advantage of people.

As the weekend wore on I knew that I had no way to tell who was good and who was bad. The specialty shop was just a couple blocks from the hotel I was in. They opened early, at 7:00AM, so I could get there and if I had to leave the car, I would be able to get a taxi to my office just a couple of miles away in time to start work by 8:30AM. So, Monday morning came and I was up early and at the auto repair shop when they opened at 7:00AM.

The owner greeted me when I walked in. I decided not to tell him what I had been told by the other shop so I could see how they diagnosed the problem. I told him the symptoms and gave him my keys. He told me to have a chair in the waiting room and he'd take a look at it to let me know if I needed to leave it.

Twenty minutes later he came in and said, "That'll be $20." I thought that wasn't bad for an estimate and I pulled $20 out of my wallet and laid it on the desk. I then asked him what was wrong and how long I could drive it before I had to get it fixed. He said, "It's fixed." I was stunned. He could see it on my face and said, "Let me guess. You took it somewhere else and they told you that such and such was broken and it would cost you $1000 - $1500 to fix it." I told him that was exactly what had happened. He said, "I don't know which shop you went to but I can tell you they know nothing about these cars. You just needed an adjustment and your car is fine." Still stunned, I said, "That's great, but I'm curious why you didn't take advantage of me." His response was priceless; "I don't think I'd get much repeat business from you, let alone referrals to your friends if I rip you off. Sure, you might not know what I fixed or adjusted, but the fact is that eventually you'd figure it out and you'd be mad. Not only would you never come back, you'd tell people I ripped you off. But if I treat you right, then you'll come back and send your friends. That's worth a lot more than one repair job where I'd make a few bucks."

Needless to say, I became a very loyal customer. And as I settled in to that city and got to know people, I did send him a lot of business. People who drive those kinds of cars get to know each other and they talk among themselves. He got lots and lots of clients because of me. He was so good at what he did that his business grew at an amazing rate as word of his expertise and honesty spread. He became known as an expert to the industry not just there locally, but around the country.

In fact, years later when I moved across the country I introduced him to a shop similar to his in the new city where I had moved. They would call and help each other with difficult problems they ran into.

That business owner was an expert and once a potential customer knew it they were drawn to him. Once they experienced working with him they wouldn't go anywhere else. They referred all their friends to him. His expertise gave him an edge over the competition. To his customers, he had no competitors. Once you did business with him you didn't even consider going elsewhere and you thought anyone who didn't do business with him was foolish.

That business owner had an edge on his competition and so can you. Once you establish yourself as the expert in your marketplace your competition can't compete.

YOU BECOME THE WORST FEAR OF YOUR COMPETITORS!

Your competition can't compete with the expert. Your expertise gives you the edge and it's no longer about price. When that new potential customer is looking for what you offer and they learn you are the expert in the community, you've got an edge that no one can take away.

Once you're the expert the loyalty of your customers builds. Your customers grow your business for you by sending you more business than ever. Potential customers are drawn to you. Your business stands out in the marketplace. You eliminate your competition because you have the ultimate marketing credibility.

How Do I Become
Known As An Expert?

Now you're probably asking how you become known as the expert. Well, it's been so effective for me that I decided to add a service in my business to help business professionals and owners achieve that goal. They can hire me to help them do it. But then, as I thought about it, I realized that many people might be like me and just want to handle it themselves. So, I decided to write this book to tell you how you can do it on your own without having to hire me to do it for you.

If you've been in your profession very long you probably have learned some things that give you more than just knowledge, they give you wisdom and insights into things you didn't learn in school or in standardized training programs. When you were in school or learning your profession there were things you were taught and they may have been very beneficial in your career. But time and experience has probably taught you things you never learn in school. Experience often teaches us far more than we ever learn in school.

When I first went to work for a large corporation I was in sales. We sold food products, mostly meat products, which were refrigerated. I went through an extensive training program for six months and learned all about the products, the industry, and sales techniques. When I completed that training I was assigned to the sales office in a major midwestern city. My first day on the job at that office I was assigned to work with an older, experienced salesman named Les. He sat me down beside him at his desk, pulled out the writing tray and placed a legal pad on it with a pen. He told me to pay attention and take notes because he was going to teach me things I had never learned in school or in the training program I'd just completed.

The first thing he taught me was an important lesson not just about that job, but that has had implications in many business situations over the years. He said to me, "Doug, I've been in this business a long time and I've learned what will make you succeed and what will kill your career. I'm going to teach you those things that will put you far ahead of other people in this job. The first thing I'm going to teach you is that your first loss is your best loss."

I really didn't understand what Les was talking about, but I kept listening. He went on saying that most of the products we sold were perishable and, whether we liked it or not, there would be times when a client would receive an incorrect order. When that happens, the product is sitting on their loading dock and needs to be sold quickly to keep it from perishing. When that would happen, the company policy required the sales rep to get approval from the corporate office on the discounted price to sell it for prior to offering it to another customer. But Les told me that when you do that the delay in waiting for the corporate office to decide on an acceptable price would cause the product to go bad. By that time a perishable product sitting on an unrefrigerated loading dock has gone bad and has no value left.

Now, you might think that was the corporate office's problem, but it wasn't. When it went bad and had to be written off it was charged against the sales rep's territory as an expense. Yes, even though the order error was not the salesman's fault, it was still charged against him for the loss. That may not be fair, but it is not uncommon in business to charge salespeople for losses. Since the profitability of our territories was a key component used in evaluating a sales rep's our performance, then it was important to the sales rep to make sure the loss was as small as possible.

Les taught me that it was better to make an educated guess at a good price and sell it quickly while the product still had value or it would hurt the profitability of the territory. Sure, the corporate office would be mad that we made a decision without them, but it was important to remember that profitability was more important than whether some person at the corporate office was upset with us.

That was a very important lesson for me, and not just for that industry. As the years have gone by and I've worked in many different industries and also had my own businesses, I've found that it is a good thing to remember that your first loss is your best loss. While the lesson in other businesses isn't directly the same, the bottom line is that time is money and it's important to move forward fairly quickly and not get bogged down in a way that would reduce profits. Sometimes we spend so much time dwelling on a problem that we invest more than it's worth.

I worked with a retailer of high-end electronics one time and they had a product that had been discontinued 3 years earlier. It had been sitting on the shelf and not sold. Finally one day a customer walked in while I was there and offered to give them $900, which was about 30% off the $1300 retail price of the product. The owner was not receptive and I took him into the back room to discuss it. I told him that he should take the money and run. He argued that it was a product with little margin and he had paid $960 for the product. That, he said, would cause him to lose money. I told him that with it sitting on his shelf for 3 years he wouldn't make money if he sold it at full retail price. He didn't understand.

I went on to explain to him that when the product wasn't selling he should have gotten rid of it as quickly as possible. Then he could have reinvested the money in a product that would sell quickly and give him turnover of his funds. By letting it sit on the shelf for 3 years he was losing because his money was tied up in a dead product and not working for him by making profits. He reluctantly agreed and sold the product to the customer. I then challenged him to pick something that was a hot item for him and invest the money in it. We tracked the new item's sales and within 2 months had turned his money 3 times at a profit. A far better thing than to have it sit there not working for him. He learned that even at a slight loss it's sometimes better to quickly get out of a product that won't sell than to sit on it and lose the ability to use that money to work for you. Understanding that your first loss is your best loss can make the best of a bad situation. Learning that lesson became one of the many things I've learned over the years that adds to my expertise.

So, you're probably saying, "Gee Doug, nice stories but what's that have to do with me?" My point is that I've picked up a few things in my working life over the years. These are the things that give a person expertise. You've had the same kinds of things happen in your life. And that knowledge is of value to your customers.

Years ago I owned a manufacturing company. The little company had national distribution and was exporting to 7 foreign countries. As we grew, it became apparent that my company needed representation in every state in the country. We couldn't just sell over the phone from a distance anymore and continue our growth rate. Our industry often worked through independent sales reps. They were known as manufacturer's representatives. They would contract with a few different manufacturers and represent each of us on a commission basis. Then they would call on prospective businesses that could use our products and offer them the variety of products they represented from all the different manufacturers.

I needed representation in two areas of the U. S., the northeast and northwest. I went to a trade show and sent word out that I was looking for representatives in those areas. My product was popular and in demand so I had no problem getting people to apply to represent my company.

As I talked to different reps I found myself interested in two rep firms that were each owned by older reps. (I was very young and these guys were in their 50s which sure seemed old to me back then!) This was an industry mostly comprised of very young people and catered to young customers, usually in their late teens, 20s and early 30s. When I hired both of these firms word got out and everyone I knew in the industry started kidding me because I'd hired such "old dinosaurs."

In hiring those two firms I ended up with four guys, two owners in each firm, who had an enormous amount of experience. I got lucky and got educated. In the years I worked with those reps not only did I get a large amount of business from them, but I also got an education that I couldn't have purchased.

Those four men taught me more than I could have dreamed. They were experts from their years of experience. They became not just my representatives, but also my go-to people for advice, insight, and education about the business. Their years in the business had taught them far more than I could have learned in any school. Chances are that your experience has given you that kind of knowledge, too.

Every person in business that has been working in their field for a reasonable period of time has had people ask them questions about the work they do. If you're a doctor or an attorney or an auto mechanic or whatever, you've most likely been asked questions. Attorneys, for example, regularly face questions from people trying to get something of value for nothing. If you own a business and know an attorney the chances are fairly good that you've asked them some simple question without actually hiring him or her to give you the answer.

If you're a doctor, I'm sure you've been asked by people for some medical advice. They've done this instead of making an appointment to come in and see you to get the answer. The same goes for most areas of business. Virtually everybody who has knowledge in business has been asked questions for which they could charge a fee.

As a business consultant I get those kinds of questions constantly. Everyone wants to know how to solve a business problem they are facing. And they ask me how to do it without hiring me to help them.

When you freely provide that kind of information you increase your value in the potential customer's eyes. The valuable information you've given them causes them to see you as an expert. That translates into business both from them and through people they refer to you because you're their expert.

Nothing has the kind of impact like that of being seen as an expert.

When I was young my father used to say you're never considered an expert unless you were in another city. His point was that it's hard for your local market to view you as an expert. And in many ways he was right, but he didn't know what I've been fortunate to learn in the ensuing years.

I've had a good career and been known as an expert by many people across the country and sometimes even in international circles. But it is true that it's usually easier to be seen as an expert when you're a good distance from home. At least that was the case until I did something to change that.

With my background, most people I've met as I've worked around the country consider me an expert. I started my first business while I was in school as a way to finance my education. And by the time I was 25 years old I had started, built and sold 3 businesses. Then I went to work for large corporations and worked my way up to executive management and was CEO of a Fortune 500 subsidiary by age 34. I have seen successes in every position in which I've ever worked, breaking both company and industry records over and over again.

I've seen the principles that I've learned and teach to others work again and again to build successes. And yet with all of that I never experienced the recognition of being an expert until I wrote a book.

When I wrote my first book it was amazing how my image went to expert status with people overnight. Even with people close to me.

With all the successes I've had in my life, it was fascinating to watch people as close as my own family not recognize it until I'd written a book. And, of course, now that I've written a few of them they consider me the expert on everything, sometimes even stuff I know little or nothing about!

My point is that getting people to think of you as an expert is not as much about what you know as it is about an image. Becoming an author makes you the ultimate purveyor of expert information. Your status as an expert soars when you have written a book.

You can become the expert in your market by authoring a book. The knowledge you've gained throughout your career makes you uniquely qualified and a book quantifies that expertise. It gives you an edge that no competitor can take away or counter. In the customer's mind you uniquely become the person who knows more, understands more, and can serve customers better. Your book validates that belief for them. That is a powerful tool to use in your marketing.

For many businesspeople marketing can be a big problem. People these days are highly sensitive to marketing. They don't want to feel pressured, or controlled and they perceive advertising as doing just that. This can pose problems when doing your marketing and trying to grow your business. Marketing is perceived by the public for some professions as unprofessional and creates resistance. When consumers see ads for doctors, attorneys, and a number of other professions they get the sense that those businesses aren't as good as others. Surveys have shown that 55%-65% of the public has that reaction. There is an unspoken attitude among the public that professionals who are good at what they do shouldn't have to advertise. Publicity from being interviewed by the media is perceived as good, but some types of marketing such as advertising are seen as bad. Remember, it is not what is true about you that matters, but what a potential customer thinks about you that matters. Their perception is their reality.

But positioning yourself as an expert is a subtle form of marketing. You're seen as the go-to business in your community. Here are some interesting points about experts:

Being an expert makes you a source of information not just for customers, but also for the media. An author can find them calling for interviews, which results in free publicity for your business.

When people are looking for a certain type of business service, all businesses that offer those services are seen as equal. The exception is when someone is known as an expert. They are in a league of their own.

When you are the expert people see you as the best choice, the trustworthy choice to do business with and, as a result, they want to do business with you.

If you are using social media to grow your business, being an expert can cause people to want to follow you. People want to be associated with "the expert" because experts get attention.

Experts are able to charge more for their services and products and make more money. The price competition is removed because you're recognized as better than the others.

Expert status that comes from being an author is not a one-time event like an advertising campaign. It gives long-term credibility because you will always be the author, the expert.

As a published author you will find things change in your life. You will become seen as an expert, possibly even a celebrity. When word gets out of your expertise you may find yourself invited to do some public speaking or consulting on your topic. You become a celebrity information source.

When you give someone a copy of your book the impression is very powerful. You aren't just some person handing them a business card. You are an expert who has a book and are sharing your expertise with them. That doesn't mean that you have to give everyone a copy. Just having a book that you can show people, that can be shown on your website and other places is a very impressive and powerful tool. The image it creates is second to none.

Where Do I Start?

Many people have desired to write a book. You might be one of them. You may even have started writing a book. But for some reason you haven't finished or the manuscript never got past being a file on your computer. Or maybe you've never even thought about writing a book until now. Whether you have thought about it or not, it's not hard to become the published author that will make you an expert in the business community.

So what do you do? Where do you start? Sure, you could hire me to write it for you. After all, that's a service I offer in my business. But you may also want to do it yourself, and I'm going to share with you just how you can.

Many people wonder how they can write a book. It seems overwhelming, like climbing a mountain. But I learned that it really is something a person can do if they set their mind to it. My first book came about after years of people telling me to write a book to help businesses. I didn't know the first thing about writing a book. Then, one day a friend whose father was a successful author gave me some pointers.

He reminded me that I always seem to have lots of stories to tell about business. He said I should write those down and file them away. Once my file was pretty full file I took them out and started organizing them. After that I did some research to support my message and started writing to bring it all together. That became my first draft of a manuscript.

It does take hard work and certainly won't write itself, but if you get organized and disciplined you can put together content for your book. I have a friend who has what I believe will be a great book in the works. He's been working on it for years and says to me regularly that his intention is to finish it "this year." Of course I've heard that now for a number of years. I know how difficult and overwhelming it can be. Discipline is the key to getting it done.

My friend doesn't understand that you can't just write here or there. It takes a plan and regular work to complete a book. A person's life changes when they decide to write a book. For most authors it means setting aside a specific time each day to write, even if it's not content for their book. Writing is an exercise that must be regular and consistent. You must get into the habit of writing and maintain it. Even on days when you can't bring yourself to writing about the topic of your book it's good to write about anything. Just exercising your writing skills is important. Plus, the more you write, the better you will get.

The most common thing people say about writing is that they don't have time. That's a common theme and it may be true. But you have to ask yourself how important it is to you. If you really want to have a marketing edge that puts you out in front of your competition, then you have to make the decision that becoming a published author is a priority.

Each person may have a different time in their schedule that works for them. Some people prefer to get up early and write for an hour or so in the morning. For others it's during a break in the day or in the evening after everything has quieted down. Some people that I know choose to do it in the middle of the night so they have quiet and there are no interruptions. I even know a few who stop virtually everything else in their lives and commit to writing until it's done. There is no "right" time except the one that works for you. But you must choose it and stick to it if you are going to succeed.

It's also important to have goals when you are writing. Only having an idea of what your book is going to be about doesn't work very well. When the goal is nebulous it's easy to not only get off track, but to waste time.

I've learned some useful things about writing. Here are a few things I've found to be helpful when working on your book:

1.) Pick a title for your book, but don't be so locked in to it that you won't change. Make it your working title with the intent to finalize it later. Often you will find that what starts out seeming like it's a good title ends up not being as good as something else once the book is finally together. The working title might become a section or chapter title, or it might be eliminated altogether. But a title is a goal so it's good to have one. It gives you something to set as your target.

2.) Write your back cover copy before you start your book. I was told this when I wrote my first book and it's very effective.

Your back cover copy is your message to someone who's interested in buying a book. It's the short little pitch that tells them what your book is about and why they should buy it. That will become your main goal as you write. And yes, it might change, too, as you go along, but not nearly as much as your title or other content. The back cover's content guides your message towards your goal.

3.) You don't have to write a long book, but it should be thorough. Cover all the ground needed and don't assume your reader understands your subject. You are the expert. They are the student. Make sure it's understandable. They should be able to explain your message once they've read your book.

4.) Be able to explain the idea of your book in one or two sentences. You might have an idea what it is as you start the book, but that may change by the time you finish.

5.) The best way to write is to develop an outline or list of bullet points to organize your thoughts and put them in order. That may be hard for some projects, but find ways to break it into parts that can be organized.

6.) Set deadlines for yourself to have each section completed. Make the deadlines concrete. Without discipline you won't complete it.

7.) Get your first draft done quickly as this will help shape where you're going. Writing is not about perfection the first time you write. Write and then rewrite. It's much easier to edit a work than to try to make each sentence and paragraph perfect the first time. In 2000 a movie was made called *Finding Forrester* in which Sean Connery plays a writer who is mentoring a young man.   In the movie Forrester (Connery's character) says to the young writer, "No thinking - that comes later. You must write your first draft with your heart. You rewrite with your head. The first key to writing is... to write, not to think!" That's pretty good advice. Just write what's on your heart the first time you write your manuscript and then when you rewrite you can use your head and start polishing, fixing, and editing.

8.) Keep your notes and ideas for your book organized so you can easily find them when writing. You may have a great idea for a part of the book you haven't written yet. Don't try to remember it but instead write it down and put it with other notes to use when the time comes. You'd be amazed how much time you waste without organization when you're trying to find that idea you had a couple of weeks or months ago.

9.) Your writing needs personality to make it something people will want to read. I have a friend who is a brilliant guy and very successful. He could teach most people in business quite a bit. His knowledge is huge, but his personality, along with his delivery, is mundane. He rattles off statistics and facts and even though it's great information, there's nothing unique in his presentation. I may not be as adept at rattling off facts and figures as he is, but I've become known for telling stories to illustrate points. People like my stories and they seem to help people understand the points I'm trying to make. Those stories are one of the main reasons that I've become a popular guest on talk shows. People want a little entertainment with their education.

10.) Write even when you don't feel like it. And write even when you don't like what you're writing. Getting it on the page to be reviewed later is a very powerful way to write. If you try to edit in your head it won't be effective and will keep some of your best ideas from ever getting to the page. You'll be amazed how often something that appears lousy to you when you are writing it turns out to be very good. Writing is much like brainstorming. Get the ideas out on the table and review them later for their worth.

11.) You don't have to write in order from the beginning to the end of your book. Often you will find that writing the sections of your outline and tying them together later is much more effective. You may even end up moving parts around. What you thought would start your book might make a great middle or end. Focus separately on each section and worry about putting them in the right order later. This also helps when you're finding yourself focused on an area of the book that is not part of what you've been working on recently. Sometimes your mind will take a little trip down a rabbit trail that is very productive. If you hold yourself rigidly to your path, determined to stay in order, you can lose those great ideas.

12.) Ask people what they think. You'll find that getting outside input can be very helpful. It gets us out of our comfort zone. Learn to accept criticism as a gift. Criticism is helpful to making what you do better. That doesn't mean all criticism is correct, but it can be eye opening. In fact, I prefer to have input be very honest and harsh. If you can set aside your feelings and not take it personally, you can learn a vast number of things that make your thinking clearer and your writing better.

13.) Along with seeking and accepting critical analysis of your work, be ready to eliminate parts of your work that you may have thought were good or important. I have a couple of books sitting in my files that are in their infancy with just some basic ideas or only have a chapter or two written. They were originally part of other books but as I worked on the other books it became clear that each of these needed to be a separate work so I moved them to a file that I might, or might not, work on later for another book. I also have thrown out many more than I've kept for other possible works. Don't be afraid to walk away from an idea. There are times when you realize that what you thought was good for content in your book just does not belong there.

Experience has taught me those points and I've found they can be very helpful as you write. Are they required? No. Are they foolproof? No. But they can be great guides to help you along your way.

When you're writing it's important to remember that when people start reading your book they are beginning a process. They are starting to have your message unveiled to them. You will need to establish a rapport with the reader. That allows you to then present your core ideas. This is earning the right to be heard.

A non-fiction book is a conversation between you and your reader. You, as the expert teacher are having a conversation with the reader, your student. And just because a person is a "student," that doesn't mean he or she is interested in the subject matter. How often were you a student in a class but weren't really interested in the subject? How the teacher begins to teach their student, or starts that conversation, will greatly impact how much the student is going to pay attention, invest himself in learning the subject matter, and apply the lessons in the process.

You could just launch into the core subject matter, but I assure you that if you do, you will be at a disadvantage. The actual approach sets up the conversation with the person, and so we need to do something to get this conversation on the right track from the beginning. If you jump right into the meat of your subject without setting things up you will be ahead of your reader—your student—and the student will be playing "catch up to the fast-talking teacher" through the entire learning process.

Never assume that your reader knows anything about what you are presenting. You are the expert, the professional. You must make sure that the people you are talking to understand what you are saying. Nothing should be taken for granted. Make it easy for them to understand. Just as the number one rule in business is to make it easy for people to do business with you, for an author your number one rule has to be making it easy for your reader to understand your message.

So how do you open this conversation effectively? You start by saying something that gets a reader's attention, is short in length, and points them in the direction you are taking the conversation. There are many ways to do this and no single one is right for every situation. You can use an analogy, tell a little story, ask a question, or whatever will work to get the point across to your student.

Find something that works for you and open your book with it to draw people in. Remember, though, that what works for one person may not work for another person.

A good example of how something that works for one person won't work for another is when you're using humor. Some people are quite natural at relating humorous or amusing stories to others. It rolls off their tongue easily and naturally and comes across as really genuine. For someone else, this isn't what they're good at doing. Have you ever met someone who just wasn't cut out to tell a joke? Maybe you're that person. If you are, then that's not the way you should introduce something. Instead you may want to point out a fact you're aware of that points the conversation in the right direction. Or maybe you would be better off sharing a quote to make a point and direct people where you're going. Find the answer that works for you.

I used a question at the beginning of my first book. I opened with: What do you think of when you hear the word "sales"? That question helped create an image in the reader's mind. I was gambling that they'd do what virtually everyone does when I ask this question—they think of the same stereotype that typifies salespeople in America. When I opened that way I got my "student" to nod in agreement.   That means I've hit common ground that we all relate to and sets up what comes next. It opens a conversation, which, in the case of sales, is a topic most people don't like, want to think about, or want to deal with. But it gets everyone on the same page and we can move forward from there.

By starting with something to get on common ground you make sure you and your reader's thoughts are moving in the same direction. You are taking nothing for granted right from the start. You do not want the reader on a different path than you're on. It's your responsibility to lead the reader.

If you've done your research and know the kinds of questions people ask you, then it's very much the same thing that a sales professional has to do with a prospective customer. They seek to find out what their prospect needs and wants before launching into a presentation. This causes the reader, like the sales professional's prospect, to tune in and listen (or read) closely. They can see that you are speaking to what interests them.

Your book should be salted with many answers to questions the reader is interested in and meets their needs. Every time you address another question you are sending a message to that reader that your goal is to help them get exactly what they want and need.

When you are doing this you hold their attention as you are educating them. You can also use this to put information in your book that supports and communicates the elevator pitch of your business. This must be done subtly because you aren't trying to sell the customer here, but you are starting to make it clear that you are an expert that can meet their needs. When you are not pushy, but subtly insert the message of what your business does and why it can meet the reader's needs it, can be very effective.

For those who aren't familiar with an elevator pitch, it is a short statement, most often not more than a couple sentences long, that says what it is that your business does. It states what makes your business unique among all the companies out there doing something similar. And in this case you would modify it slightly so that it is just informative and not a sales pitch. You are only educating the customer to reinforce to them what you do and that you are the expert.

An elevator pitch is succinct. It's called an "elevator pitch" because it has to be something that, if you were in an elevator with someone, you could state it in those few seconds you are with that person and have the person interested enough to want to know more about your business.

When I'm working on an elevator pitch (some people call it a "USP" or "Unique Selling Proposition") with a consulting client in my business, I tell him or her to picture getting on an elevator with me and handing me their business card. The person now has one minute or less to say something that will cause me to want to call them back so they can learn more about their business once they get off the elevator at the end of that minute. This means it has to be something that makes your business unique. It is something that creates in the listener a desire to want to know more.

An elevator pitch answers the key question: What does my business do better and differently than my competitors'? That's exactly what you should be promoting as your expertise.

As you work your way through writing your book you can add some additional information that will reinforce your claim to expertise. The best way to do this is to use stories or examples. When people read that you have actually done the things you're talking about it gives you more credibility.

Keeping those things in mind will help you as you put your book together.

It's Written,
Now What Do I Do?

Being an author isn't as hard as many people think. The hardest part has always been getting your book published. Today, even that isn't as hard as it used to be. There are now many ways for an author to get their work published. Let's go through some common options and their advantages and disadvantages.

You can try to get published by the large publishing houses whose names we've all seen on books. There are also smaller publishers who offer opportunities. Most of the large publishers find their authors through author's agents. Few authors work directly with these publishers.

The large publishers receive thousands of manuscripts per week (4000 – 5000 is common). Because the number is so large, most publishers will not accept a manuscript that is unsolicited. Few people who send their manuscript to a publisher actually get anyone to look at it, let alone read it. Most are either thrown in good old file 13 (the wastebasket) or simply returned unread to the sender.

As of June 2013 there were 12,703 bookstores in America. There are between 300,000 and 500,000 books published each year. Add to that the millions of books already in print and no store could stock all of the new titles each year, let alone those that already are available.

Few books sell well enough to cover their costs. This has caused publishers to only give them a short time to prove their saleability. It means they keep them in print a short time, usually available about four to six months in stores and after that still available in print for a year. Most books are very low volume in sales, usually less than a few thousand copies are sold. The business of publishing is not the panacea people have come to think it is.

Publishers are not out there throwing money at new authors trying to get their work published. Contrary to what Hollywood shows us on TV and in the movies, few authors receive advances. Unless the author is famous, such as former presidents or other public figures, the chances of receiving a big advance are slim.

Most authors receive no advances and the royalties paid are small. For those that do receive advances they are required to pay it back within a set period of time if their book doesn't sell enough copies to cover the costs incurred by the publisher.

Additionally, these days authors are expected to pay for the marketing costs of their book. The publisher doesn't pay to promote them, the author does. I've heard many stories where authors have invested tens of thousands of dollars, sometimes over $100,000 to market their book, often making a sacrifice of their retirement savings in hope of a big payoff. Sadly, few have success enough to recoup their costs.

If all that isn't bad enough, the large publishers very rarely consider an author that is not represented by an agent (another expense the author incurs). Add to that the fact that your chance of getting traction without a publicist, a PR consultant, is virtually impossible unless you're lucky enough to have done something that gets you significant press attention. The costs of a good PR consultant can be astronomical. It is not uncommon for them to require payments of $10,000 per month to represent you.

If you're lucky enough to make it through all of that, usually the author is required to relinquish the copyright to their work. That means that they have no say in any changes that are made to the book, but their name stays on it. If changes are made the author is bound by contract to live with them. The author loses all control of their work and cannot use it elsewhere without contractual permission from the publisher.

Not only is the process painful, it is unnecessary for what you are trying to accomplish with your book. The purpose for you is not to sell lots of books in bookstores. The purpose is to get a book published and use it to give you credibility as an expert in your field. The book that makes you an expert becomes the best way to get someone into your sales funnel so you can begin to guide them through the buying process.

You only need to be able to show a professionally finished product that is sold on Amazon.com, the world's largest bookseller, to have credibility. You don't have to have a major publisher's name on your book to have credibility. The physical book with a listing on Amazon.com will be enough to prove your expertise.

That's where the new methods that are available today for publishing come in. You can now publish a book yourself and do it for a very affordable price.

Publishing your book on your own is not new. Many famous authors have done it. John Grisham and Stephen King today and in the past Edgar Allen Poe, Mark Twain, and Zane Grey are all examples of those who have done it. By publishing yourself you retain control of your work. You keep the copyright and control of your work along with every step of the process. You deal with the editor, the cover designer, the person who does your book layout, and the printer. Having no middleman gives you complete control.

Doing this in the past often meant printing and production quality that was questionable, delays in getting things done, and significant commitment of money to purchase hundreds or thousands of books for future sale that authors ended up storing in their basement or garage. Most of those books would end up sitting there for years gathering dust while the author tried to figure out how to recoup their investment.

Not anymore. Today you can have your book published and printed on demand so that you don't have to buy a whole bunch of books in advance. You can order as few as one book at a time and get it quickly. Technically you never have to order any books, other than proof copies to review when it's being produced.

As a businessperson I'm sure that you can appreciate being able to have something available with no money being tied up in inventory. That frees up your capital for other uses in your business. But, once again, the purpose of the book is not as much to sell a large number of them. It is to have the credential of being an author, which gives you the ultimate marketing credibility when you're seen as an expert.

The Steps To Production

Editing

Before you are ready to produce a book, it has to be written well. Today's society often doesn't care about misspellings, lack of proper grammar and punctuation, and other writing problems when they write. And while much of this is driven by both the dumbing down that has occurred through our school systems and social media, it's not acceptable when you're writing a book. When people are reading they see those kinds of errors as sloppy and are distracted by them.

Recently I was meeting with a client and we were talking about copy for his website. He had written his own content and was sure it was "good enough" without having me offer my professional copywriting services to make it shine. We talked about some typos and grammar issues and he said, "Doug, today people don't care about that stuff anymore. In fact, I think it shows you're more human if you have a few errors. I think people are drawn to the genuineness of it. You're being too picky."

I told him that not only was he wrong, but even if people didn't care about it, it still harmed his marketing. With a puzzled look on his face he asked why. I went on to tell him that if you are trying to get a message through to someone it is very important that you get their undivided attention.

If someone comes into your business and you are trying to talk to them about the services or products you offer and you are continually interrupted while talking to the person, they will be distracted from what you are trying to communicate. Your chances of getting the message that you are trying to communicate through to that customer are miniscule.

The same happens when someone is reading what you've written. Things like grammar, punctuation and misspellings are a distraction and take the concentration of the reader from what you are trying to tell them. It is very important to do everything you can to avoid distractions. That will allow them to focus on your message.

Now, that said I should warn you that when my first book was published I was warned that no matter how many times you proofread it, no matter how many people proofread it, it is rare not to end up with some typo or problem in the final production copy. My first book was in its 2nd printing, having had many, many people read it, and no one ever found that one quotation mark was in the wrong place and a period in another part of the book was missing. Then, while having coffee with a friend one day he said he'd just read the book and found the missing period. A year later I happened to find the quotation mark error myself.

I do a lot of reading in my work and you'd be amazed how often I find errors in the work of professionals. There is not a week that goes by that I don't find at least a couple of errors in professionally written and published materials. As a successful author I know said to me, no matter how many times you go over it, there always seem to be some errors that slip through.

Errors do happen and they're not the end of the world. But you certainly want to avoid as many as possible. What is the best way to do it? If you are not a professional at it and want to have the best chance at an error-free book it is best to hire a good book editor. They not only look for these kinds of errors, but they will help you learn how to write better. They will help make your book easier to read. They clean things up, polish things, and make you look better as an author.

A good book editor is like a great chef. You may be a wonderful cook, but a great chef can come in and add those little extra things to the meal to make it really stand out as special. They know just what is needed to make that meal perfect. A good book editor is much the same. You don't have to use an editor, but they can offer a huge advantage in making your book shine.

Front Cover

Once your book is complete, you will need to start bringing all the pieces together to have a finished book. The first impression you make is important.

A lot of people today would argue that how we present ourselves isn't important, but after 39 years in business I've learned that the first impression you make is not only important, it may be the only chance you get to win a person over. In my book, *You Sold Me At Hello: How to Get People to Buy Without Being a Salesman*, I explain that you have 10 words or 10 seconds to win someone over or you lose your opportunity. I've reprinted that chapter of my book below addressing the issue of first impressions:

You've Got 10 Words or Ten Seconds

When you have first contact with your prospect you must remember that your first impression is critical. My father was known around the country as a successful businessman and world-class sales trainer. He taught me many of the key elements of business success that I've used throughout my life. He repeatedly would say to me, "You've got 10 words or 10 seconds to win or lose a prospect when you meet them. Don't blow it."

What he meant by that was that the first words you say and the first thing the person sees will affect whether your relationship goes any further. People will tune you out quickly. Usually you have a little more than ten words or ten seconds, but not much more.

That problem was even harder for me early in my career. At that time I did not look old enough to be taken seriously as a businessperson. I sure don't have that problem anymore! I remember calling my father one day and telling him I had trouble getting credibility because I looked so young.

My father worked with people in some youthful industries. He'd colored his hair for years to retain his youthful look in a young industry. So I expected him to say, "Get some gray hair dye and you'll look older. That will fix it." But he didn't. He said, "You're always too young until you're too old. Enjoy it while you've got it."

Boy, I didn't get that! I told him how I'd show up for appointments and be stopped by the receptionists who would demand an I.D. to prove I was old enough to be there. That was very embarrassing! And my own father, the man who had started me in selling and could sell better than anyone I knew, only told me to enjoy it!

I pressed him for a better answer and even suggested that I add gray coloring to my hair. He told me that I could do that, but what he suggested was something else. He told me that he knew that I always knew my products well. He told me I had to become the expert in my field. Knowledge, he told me, was a valuable tool.

Then he told me that developing a short opening presentation that would get the prospect's attention and hold it would be far more effective.

I thought about it and realized that he was right, but I wanted to do more. I started studying my product. I became the person that people went to when they wanted more information. I was the expert. I was their reference point when they wanted to know more.

Then I developed an effective opening statement. But that wasn't enough. I had another idea.

I had always liked dressing well. I found that it gave me credibility. When I was young I spent a great amount of the money I earned on clothes. I decided to dress so well that prospects would take notice. I started spending as much as I could afford for the best clothes available.

Then one day I was working in a large city and had some time in my schedule between appointments. I was in an affluent area that I wasn't familiar with so I drove around a bit. I found myself in a shopping center, stopping at a drugstore to pick up something for a headache. After I got back to my car I looked up and down the strip mall at the different stores. I noticed a thrift store. I decided to take a look. I'd never been in a thrift store in a high-class neighborhood and I wondered if it would be different than the Goodwill and Salvation Army stores I'd been in before.

I wandered in and noticed right away that the clothes on the racks weren't the same quality as I had seen in other thrift stores. These were very nice clothes. I wandered over to the men's suits. I found that they had very expensive suits with virtually no wear. A lady who worked there came over and asked if she could help me.

I commented about the quality of the clothes and she smiled and said, "You know, it's amazing what we get in here. This neighborhood is so affluent and people here only wear things a few times and donate them to us. You can find some remarkable things in here."

She was right. I was looking at a suit identical to one I had seen at a high-end department store earlier in the week. This was about thirty-five years ago—and the department store had the suit priced at $800. That was a lot of money for a suit for a young guy in those days. But the one in the thrift store was in absolutely perfect condition and it was only $35! All it needed was to have the pants hemmed up and the sleeves shortened a bit and it would fit perfectly. Immediately I bought it.

I got home, took it to the dry cleaners and tailor, and when I got it back I had a new suit for a price that was unbelievable. Now I could walk in to an office and look like a million bucks. Because I looked the part, I had instant credibility.

I found myself frequenting that thrift store for many years. Many of the suits must have come from the same guy because it seemed that many I bought had the same fit and needed the same alterations. I never met him, but whoever this man was, he gave me an edge early in my career. Over the years my successes increased and I moved around the country. As I bought new clothes I no longer shopped at the thrift store. But I did continue to purchase high quality, well cut clothes and to be very careful with my image. I believe that this is still important for people today.

Yes, society has gotten more casual. And while that's probably to our detriment, as along with losing the formality we seem to have also lost our manners and respect. It's hard to find common courtesy anymore. But that's a topic for another book. Even if you work in Silicon Valley where shorts and flip-flops are frequently accepted, you can always step slightly above the norm. You don't have to dress like you're going to a black tie event to dress well. Be clean, neat, and sharp. It will make a difference.

It is interesting that recently business attire has been moving back to more formal attire, though. Leading fashion consultants and department stores are seeing things move away from the casual. Menswear sections of stores are carrying more suits and ties and women's fashions are moving in a similar direction toward formality again. Even in the casual sector we are seeing companies expect more than jeans and t-shirts. The most casual of business environments are now setting standards such as sport jackets and shirts, khakis or dress slacks, and nice shoes for men. For women, we are seeing companies prohibiting such clothing as shorts, skirts, and tops that are too casual and flip-flops on their feet.

How does this affect the sales professional? It means we need to be careful what we wear. You may not dress up as much as salespeople did during the main part of my career, but you can still look good.

You should dress like someone that your client would go to for advice. Don't forget, if you are with a client who is wearing casual clothes and the owner or president of the company comes in and interrupts the meeting, will you be dressed as well or better than the boss? You should be. If you dress that way and the boss shows up, then you are ready to meet with him or her and can do so on an equal footing.

Trust me: You may not think how you dress will affect how your presentation is received, but I can tell you it does. It may not change the way you make the presentation, but it will affect how what you say is perceived by the people you are with. Knowing how to dress in a situation will impact the outcome and is as much a part of your homework as anything else. You want to make an impression. You've got ten seconds—don't blow it.

I've worked with people who say that what they wear doesn't matter. They're going to be their own person and no one will tell them how to dress. Such an attitude hurts their business. I have done business with people in industries ranging from construction to banking, from small retail shops to Fortune 500 companies. I've always found that looking professional, like someone that a person would go to for advice, helps in gaining credibility. When you look like an expert, people give you credit for being one (And sometimes even when you're not!).

Years ago I got a referral into a successful yacht-building business. No one in the company wore anything but casual clothes. Most everyone usually wore shorts to work, even the owner. He loved boats and being around boats. He had built a very successful business and formality was not very important to this guy. He loved the idea of being able to live his casual lifestyle all the time. He was proud of it and felt it was a mark of his success.

The person who referred me to him knew how I dressed and told me how casual the business. It didn't change my approach and I went to the appointment in my usual suit and tie. I was young but very good at my presentation and I won the interest of the owner. He invited me back for a second meeting. The process was long and continued through more meetings until finally he bought from me.

I sold employee benefit packages (things like retirement plans, etc.) and once we'd signed the contract we set up a meeting with all of his employees so I could tell them about their new benefits. This was in Florida in the middle of the summer. It was high humidity and 95 degrees in the hot sunshine outdoors. I showed up in a dark blue suit and tie.

The meeting was going well, questions from the employees were good, and interest was high. We were having a good time and the people were very attentive.

The owner interrupted me about half way through my presentation. He apologized as he took the microphone from me in front of the crowd that numbered a couple hundred. He looked at his employees and said, "I don't know about you guys, but it's hot today!"

Everyone laughed and then he looked at me saying, "Doug, we really appreciate what you're doing here and how professional you are, but would you please take off your coat? Because I'm about to faint from the heat just watching you."

Everyone laughed and so I took off my coat, which resulted in a lot of applause. It was the first time I'd ever done that at a business appointment. Later he told me that he appreciated that even though his company was a casual business, I'd always taken the time to look and act professionally. He said that was one of the factors that caused him to choose to do business with me over my competitors.

I had an assistant with me at the meeting. When we got back to the office she told everyone in the office what had happened. People were shocked. I didn't even take my coat off at the office. I got a lot of ribbing from my fellow workers, but it was all in good fun and as the story traveled through the company it reinforced to every person how much my attire was a part of my professionalism.

The next year we moved to a new office. The day we moved, I came in from some appointments and was helping get stuff organized. And my secretary was trying to get the wires for her computer hooked up. The wires had to run under the desk and she wasn't sure what to do because she'd worn a dress to work that day.

I told her I'd take care of it, so I took off my coat and crawled under her desk to run the wires. As I fiddled with the wires under that desk for a few minutes I heard a commotion. I came out from under the desk to find all thirty-six people that worked in my office standing around watching.

I asked what they were doing and someone spoke up. "Doug, we all had to see this. We've never seen you take your coat off at work."

Once again it caused some laughter but my professional image was appreciated, respected, and some even envied it. It was an image that paid off both with my fellow workers and my clients.

Don't take lightly how you dress. It is very important. The rewards of a good first impression will be powerful.

My goal in business has always been to win. And in the end, if I get you to buy from me, then I win. So, I have to ask myself, what is important to me, and what isn't?

I happen to like to dress well, but some people insist on wearing casual clothes. Here's an example of how what you wear can affect your success: I know a guy who tries hard to be successful at selling, but he does not seem to do much better than just survive. He is adamant that he only dresses in t-shirts and jeans. He says it isn't important how he dresses and that it doesn't make a difference in the quality of work he does. I've tried to tell him that while what he says may be true about the quality of his work, there are people who will have less consideration or even respect for him because of how he dresses. He does not understand that how you dress sends a message to a customer. When you dress nicely it says, "I want to be here and you are important to me." He is so determined to be his own boss and have no one tell him what to do that he hurts his success because of it.

But just understand this: We make choices that affect our business. It's not about whether what someone thinks about you is right or wrong, it's about increasing your chances to do more business. Isn't that what we want? We need to consider the price we'll pay, the consequences, when we choose to do something that may have an impact just how successful we may be.

We have to be cognizant of things that can affect our success and decide how we want to handle them.

This is not to judge any of you and the choices you make. It is to help you make good decisions about the choices you make that may impact your business.

Remember how I said we should seek criticism so we can grow? If you have feelings that are easily hurt or you're easily offended, you need to deal with that. It will affect your ability to grow and succeed. We learn more from criticism and rejection than we ever will if we won't learn from criticism.

And when it comes to things like our appearance, our presentation, our ability, our knowledge, or other things that are affecting how people receive us, we have to decide whether it is more important to do things our way or if it's worth giving them up so we can obtain more success. I'm sure I could have done very well over the years if I had chosen to dress more casually, but I am also sure I wouldn't have done as well. Even if I didn't care to dress the way I did, I would have chosen to do it if it would give me a better chance at success.

I want to try to try to "stack the deck" in my favor as much as possible. I am confident you do, too.

———————————————

Ten words or ten seconds means your first impression is critical to your success. This last section that I included from my sales book showed how that's true in the personal sense, the same goes with your book. The cover is very important when you want to make an impression to reinforce your image as an expert.

Don't let criticism bother you. See it as a friend that wants to help you be your best.   The goal is to make your book as effective as possible, so you should want your book cover to be as effective as possible.

The cover is what sells your book, both when someone is considering buying it, and when it sells the initial credibility of the book when someone sees it. That doesn't mean it has to be serious or solemn. Rather, it must be persuasive with a message that draws people to it. I remember hearing a few years ago that if the cover of a book doesn't draw people to it, then there is little chance the person will consider it any further.

A great way to get ideas for covers is to go to a bookstore and look at books, in the section that would include your book. See which covers stand out and which ones draw you to them. You might even want to bring a few friends or ask people browsing in the store for their opinions. Then, make a list of a variety of those books.

Go home and look them up on your computer at a site like Amazon.com. Put together a list of the online links to those books and then send an email to at least ten friends and family members asking them to choose their three favorite covers and to tell you the order of their preference and why they chose those covers. When you get their responses make a spreadsheet or list of which covers came up on top. You will most likely find that some covers were frequently chosen than others. That gives you an idea of which designs draw people to them.

You shouldn't directly copy someone else's cover. Many of those have copyrights or trademarks and you'd be violating them if you just copied them. But they can give you ideas for colors, layout, and design. I wouldn't stop there, though. To really make it work for you your best bet for a great cover is to hire a cover designer. They may come up with an entirely different idea than what your little survey revealed, but they may also take the information and develop something along those same lines that will work for you.

Good cover designers can make your book shine. They will give it a personality that makes it stand out so that when people see it they are drawn to it. Your book may have a solemn, serious cover, or it may have a whimsical cover, or it may end up with something entirely different than you can imagine. The creativity of a good designer can do things for you with even the simplest of elements so that it makes a powerful difference.

I remember when I wrote my first book I had done a ton of research and knew what I wanted. My publicist and editors liked my ideas and I knew that I was on a good track but I don't have the artistic flair that could really make it what it needed to be. I found a cover designer who was great. She liked my idea and went to work on it. Within a short time she brought back a sample that was slightly changed but dramatically better. She had brought it to life. It was a simple cover, but her choice of curves and angles in the geometric design along with great fonts really made the book stand out.

We're all specialists at certain things. A good cover designer can be as big a gift to your book as you are to your clients.

Back Cover

Remember that tip I gave you to write your back cover copy first, thereby giving you a goal to write to? When you are writing that copy there are a few things you should remember. First, the back cover copy is very effective if you start with a headline or quote from the book itself. If it's a quote, obviously you may end up adding that when you're near completion of your manuscript. The headline or quote is something that anyone who picks up the book will use to determine if they want to look further.

Follow that headline with a description of the book contents that include important points about what the reader will find inside. Often this will be the very same copy you use for your listing on Amazon.com. These are the points that are the key things readers will get from reading your book.

At the end of the copy it's important that you have a short paragraph that clearly and succinctly tells the reader why this book is important for them to read. This is where you're asking for the order, closing the sale.

International Standard Book Number

You will also need an International Standard Book Number (ISBN) for your book. You can go to Bowker.com and purchase one. This is what identifies your book to all in the book world. This is an exclusive identifier that will be for your book only. It is what identifies the title, author, publisher, etc. A Bar Code will also be necessary on the back cover. It is used to identify the ISBN through scanning technology.

Interior Layout

You will need to hire someone who can do the layout of your book. Often called Book Designers, their job is to lay out the interior of your book so it is ready for the printer. This is no minor issue. A book that doesn't look right is a turnoff to the reader. It loses its professional appeal. A Book Designer makes sure the book looks right on the page. They work to avoid things like having a chapter end with the last word being all alone by itself on a page. Correct line spacing, good choice of font style and size, page number placement, chapter title placement, conversion of files from word processor formats to the required formats of printers, etc. All of the things that make a book look "right" to the reader are addressed by Book Designers.

After I'd written my first book I was asked by a publicist to help a potential client of hers get his book published. She felt I could offer insights another writer might appreciate. It was a science fiction novel, which was quite a distance from non-fiction business writing that I'd done, but she wanted to show this author the ins and outs of working with publishers compared to an author choosing to self-publish.

I spoke with the author after he sent me a copy of his book. It was self-published. The story was riveting. This guy clearly had talent and took me from total ignorance of his topic to driving my curiosity and interest in the subject.

But there was also a problem. As I read the book it just felt odd. Something about the book wasn't right. Not only did this author desperately need an editor to clean up and polish his writing, he needed a Book Designer to make his book look like a real book. This thing looked like something he'd had printed by a local printer whose business was not book publishing. It looked homemade. I'm not talking about the cover, but about the interior of the book. The cover was simple and without impact. But the interior felt wrong when you read it.

After I read the book I met with him and commended him for writing a story that was able to capture the attention of someone like me who had never had interest in the subject. I also made recommendations both as a fellow-author and as a specialist in marketing.

He was very resistant. He was sure he didn't need an editor, even though I pointed out numerous grammatical and punctuation errors, in addition to typos. I also tried to show him his back cover copy did nothing to draw a reader's interest. Even his title was weak, at best. His overall content was good, but he needed professional help to make the book great. He insisted that his book would be a huge success and that he would get a movie deal as soon as someone in Hollywood saw it. Boy was he dreaming! But he thought he was the next superstar author for which the world was waiting.

After a few meetings it was apparent he wouldn't accept any input or advice. I told him his ego was hurting his future and then I walked away knowing that his ego was in the way of his success. He didn't seem to care and discontinued working with the publicist, too.

A couple years later I happened to meet the publicist he ended up using. He hadn't changed anything but had spent huge sums of money trying to market his book. The new publicist informed me that even though he'd sent dozens and dozens of copies to movie contacts in Hollywood and also to various publishers, he was not able to get anyone interested. The book just looked so unprofessional that no one would give it a chance. They assumed the book's content was as poor as it's look. The first impression it made hurt instead of helped.

Could he have gotten a movie deal for his book? Possibly, if he'd been willing to make his book read well and look like a professionally produced book. But his rigid resistance to seeking help killed any chance he had for opportunity. The new publicist let me know that the author had spent a great deal of money, tens of thousands of dollars, trying to get his book off the ground and had no success.

You've got ten words or ten seconds to make an impression. Your book needs to look professional if you're going to make the right impression.

.

Getting Your Book Printed

There are a variety of options available for getting your finished book printed. I've looked at and dealt with a variety of them. My purpose in this book was not to give you a huge list of options for you to wade through, but rather to give you information that is the result of what I've learned and what has worked well for me. After all, you don't need to go through the learning curve that I did.

Once you have all the aforementioned things handled you will still need to get your book printed and also put on Amazon.com. You might even want to have availability of your book to bookstores in America and possibly other countries. After all, just because this is being done for the purpose of making you stand out as an expert in your field and give you the ultimate marketing credibility doesn't mean that you might not want to see if you can sell a few of these books, too. And doing so is just a matter of knowing how to get good distribution.

When I first became an advocate of self-publishing I talked to so many people. I learned about going to printers to have books printed and learned about having to stock them myself and handle all marketing and shipping. Then I learned about some printers who do what's known as print on demand printing. In that method your files are given to the printer who will print them as you need them. You can order as little as one book at a time. And, the best part was that they would even drop ship the books for me to whomever I specified.

Compared to the idea of having to print, pay for, stock and ship a lot of books, the print on demand model really makes it easy and cost effective to get a book on the market.   All an author has to do is supply them with digital files that are ready to print and in some cases pay a few fees.

After speaking to a variety of people, and doing more research than I probably needed to, I learned that a great print on demand company is Lightning Source (Lightningsource.com).   They are located in Tennessee and may be some of the nicest people with which I've ever dealt.   And, they are part of Ingram, one of the largest book distributors in the country so they have distribution options that can give your book distribution like that of the major publishers.

If you sign up for the right options with Lightning Source they will have your book available through their catalog to most bookstores in the United States.   Plus they have additional distribution options to many foreign countries and they will get your book on Amazon.com and BarnesAndNoble.com, too.   Their fees vary depending on what services of theirs that you choose.

If you desire great distribution to have your books available in many places, then Lightning Source is a good choice. For example, in America virtually all bookstores have the Ingram catalog and can order the books they produce. That means that even though a store may not stock it, if anyone were to go to that store and ask for it the store could order it just like books from the major publishing houses.

I never expected to sell my books in places outside the U. S., but between my television and radio broadcast appearances and Lightning Source's distribution options I've been surprised at the people in places like Canada, Australia, Great Britain, Japan, and other countries that have requested my books.

I have used Lightning Source for some of my books and been very satisfied. They are a good choice for an author who wants to get their book published and not have to invest in a huge inventory or handle the distribution issues.

The other option that is available is Createspace.com, a division of Amazon.com. They also publish using a print on demand model. They offer some additional services like editing, book design, etc., although I have a preference for outside sources to handle those things. And they have some expanded distribution available, too. While I like them, there is a definite difference using them versus a company like Lightning Source.

When using them you do have some expanded distribution options available, but you lose the opportunity of having your book on other websites like BarnesAndNoble.com. However, with Amazon.com controlling the largest market share those other sites may not be as important to you. I first used Createspace.com for a large print version of one of my books and was very satisfied.

Whether you choose Lightning Source or Createspace, you set the retail price for your book. However, with Lightning Source you also control the wholesale selling price and thereby control your profit more than you can with Createspace. Either are good choices, it just depends on what you're looking for when shopping for a company to handle your printing and distribution needs.

Your Other Option

As you consider what it will take to write a book you may be wondering if there are any other ways to accomplish this task. After all, you are a busy person and adding another project with a new and separate learning curve just doesn't seem to fit your schedule. The answer to whether there is another way to accomplish writing your book is yes and no.

Basically there are 3 ways to write a book:

1.) Write it yourself - Using the tips I gave you early in this book you can write a very effective book.

2.)   Record it and have it transcribed so you can then edit and complete it - If you record your book content you can have a transcriptionist type up everything you've said on the recording. Whether it's a speech you gave, a lecture, a seminar, an interview, or just you rambling on into a microphone as you wade through the ideas, it can be turned into a written document that you then only have to organize, clean up, fill in the gaps and edit it.

Another way to get it transcribed is to use transcription software such as Dragon Naturally Speaking for Windows or Dragon Dictate for Mac. These programs allow you to speak into a microphone and have your word processing program (such as Microsoft Word) type automatically for you. The only problem with using these products is that they only work when you are talking into the microphone. You can't use Dragon with recordings you have made previously to get them transcribed.

You should also be aware that the software does have a learning curve both for the user and the software itself. It will do pretty good when you start, but it takes time for it to adapt to your speech patterns so its accuracy gets better over time. It will give you a rough document where you can then go back and organize, clean up and change things.

3.) Hire a ghostwriter - As you've read through this book you may like the idea of putting yourself way out in front of your competition by being seen as the expert, but you just can't find the time nor do you want to deal with the hassles that come with writing a book yourself. You've got a business to run and adding this project to your schedule is just not possible. While building your business is critically important to success, sometimes we have to find ways to do things without giving up the time we need for other things.

An option to get a book written without the same investment of time that writing it yourself involves would be to hire someone to ghostwrite your book.

Whether you realize it or not, many books are not written by their authors. They are written by ghostwriters who are hired to wade through information supplied by the author to create a book for them.

Ghostwriters work from various sources of information including interviews they do with the author, articles and other materials written by the author, recordings of lectures, speeches, and other ways the ideas have been presented on the subject by the author, etc.

This isn't a question of talent. You may be very talented in many areas, but that doesn't mean that writing is for you. You are simply trying to share your expertise with an audience and a ghostwriter can help you get that done. Ghostwriters get your message into the form of a book and agree to allow you to have your name exclusively on the book.

The cost of a ghostwriter depends on a number of factors but is offset by the time you save so you can run your business. This can be an effective method to accomplish your goal of establishing yourself as an expert and giving you ultimate marketing credibility.

When I saw the impact that becoming a published author had on my credibility and reputation as an expert, even in my own family, I only wished I had written my first book sooner. It truly does make you stand out from your competition.

For me, since I've done fairly well at writing, enjoy it, and have won some awards for my writing, it seemed only natural to offer ghostwriting services as part of my business. After all, as a business consultant my entire business is about making other people's businesses successful. What could be better than to offer to them what has been very effective for me?

So, you do have the option of having me ghostwrite it for you.

Don't continue being just another business in your field. Show people you're the expert by using the Ultimate Marketing Tool to get ultimate marketing credibility. Then you can stand out in the marketplace and eliminate your competition.

About the Author

Doug Johnson is an author, public speaker, and business consultant. Doug has been interviewed by such magazines as Success, websites such as Careerbuilder.com, and on radio and television shows in the U.S. and Canada, Europe, Australia, New Zealand, Asia, Israel and the Middle East.

Doug's award-winning books have won him the Best New Sales Advice Book Award and the 50 Great Writers You Should Be Reading Award.

For 39 years Doug has worked helping all sizes and types of businesses.

A few facts about his background:

- He was promoted to management in a large international company while working when he was still in high school.

- He started his first business while in school to finance his education.
- By the time he was 25 years old he had started, built, and sold three businesses.
- He went to work in corporate America working his way up through executive management and by age 34 he was CEO of a Fortune 500 subsidiary.
- He has worked with a wide variety of industries and markets throughout the U.S. and seen the business methods he uses work in every one of them.

Contact Information

Doug Johnson is available for consulting, speaking engagements, and workshops.

Here's how to reach him:

Email:
DougJohson@HorseSenseConsulting.com
     (email address is not case sensitive)

Mail:
P. O. Box 88114
Black Forest, CO 80908

Website:
www.HorseSenseConsulting.com
     (web addresses are not case sensitive)

Hi! My name is dehanna and it's my job to help you create...

Services include:

- Full-Color Covers
- Interior Layout
- Ebooks
- Shepherding
- Editing
- Writing & Art

Online at:
www.EditWriteDesign.com

Dehanna Bailee has more than ten years experience in both the traditional and independent publishing industries. Clients include everything from hobbyists to seasoned pros. Her personal work has been recognized and/or recommended by notable sources such as SPAWN, Dan Poynter, Preditors & Editors, and Writers Digest Magazine.